TABLE OF CONTENTS

Introduction

Are you trying to achieve those goals that you've set for yourself and your business, but you often feel that there is not enough time in the day for you to achieve your goals? No matter how hard you try, you always feel as though you're not moving forward with your goals.

Regardless of what industry you are in, learning how to efficiently manage your time is one of the most important skills that will change your life and set you on the path of success.

Without having a set plan to make sure each hour that you spend on your business is spent effectively, you'll struggle to meet your deadlines, follow through on product launches and prioritize the most important thing to your business.

Don't worry, we have got you covered. In this book, we will take you through everything you need to know about how to use your time efficiently, be more productive and reach your goals as a result.

The strategies discussed in this book are developed to help you learn to use your time effectively, make sound decisions about the kind of work you prioritize, and achieve success.

So, without further ado, let's dive in!

Change Your Mindset

One of the main reasons why a lot of people don't get success in their business is pure because of the way they manage their time to do their daily tasks.

And that one problem is:

"They need to stop think like an employee and start thinking like an entrepreneur"

They're so stuck to the 9-5 mentality that they are unable to adapt to the entrepreneurial mindset. If they adapt to the entrepreneurial mindset, it will help them to train themselves to focus on the most important tasks of the day by prioritizing their time and assigning value to the time they spend building their business.

As an entrepreneur, your time is more valuable than it has ever been. You no longer work for someone else and get paid for each working day regardless of the results. If you aren't focusing on the most important tasks efficiently, you can easily fall behind your competitors.

As an entrepreneur, you're solely responsible for your business, so your ability to value your time and make every minute count will have a major impact on how successful your business will be.

If you don't make this important change in your mindset, then you'll always struggle to get to where you want your business to be.

Fortunately, it's not rocket science to break that cycle and change your mindset to be that of a business owner. It begins with preparing yourself for the realities of being a business owner.

Time is Money

You can achieve this by:

Setting Realistic Deadlines: You must be honest about your realistic capacity of getting stuff done each day. Then you need to decide the number of hours you're willing to invest in your business each day and then assign that time to specific tasks in priority order.

Task Breakdown: Task breakdown is also referred to as "sub-tasking". We'll talk more about the importance of sub-tasking in a bit because it's a great way to boost your productivity and get more done in less time.

Avoid Distractions. Your working environment will change a lot from what you may be used to as an employee, and you need to optimize your workspace so that it's supporting a focused and productive workflow.

Why are you procrastinated?: This is one of the hardest things to acknowledge at times, especially if you've gotten into the habit of procrastinating for reasons you aren't aware of.

We'll discuss more this in an upcoming chapter because it is a very important step.

Be Ruthless in Prioritizing. Does your email need to stay open while you work so that all those notifications cause you to continuously check your inbox?

Avoiding distractions, as we just mentioned above, plays a huge role in your ability to prioritize. Every minute needs to count and you'll get a lot more done if you focus each segment of your time on a single task.

In the next chapter, we'll take a closer look at how you can learn the "sub-tasking" technique, which will immediately boost your daily output and keep you focused to meet your goals.

Sub Tasking

For several years, I started my day doing multiple different things at once. I'd check email, then maybe do some scripting for my videos, then head over to social media, and repeat the cycle.

This vicious cycle cost me valuable time, and while I thought I was good at multitasking, the truth is everyone will struggle to get everything done if they're trying to do everything at once.

Sub Tasking is where you decide to focus on just one major task at a time (or even per day). Depending on the type of business you're involved in, this might include one day exclusively focused on graphic design, then one day dedicated to web designing.

Consider creating a detailed task list of all the important aspects of your business; the things that keep it all afloat and require your time.

This can be tricky because we tend to think all things are important but they're not.

When it comes to any business, there are a handful of critical tasks that need to be taken care of daily, and the rest just adds a little more gas to the tank. They can be done later once the main tasks are out of the way.

You need to learn to place a value on every ounce of "fuel" you have left. That's where sub-tasking comes into play.

By focusing on one main task a day, or at least per segment of the allocated time, you are not only able to focus strictly on getting it done on time but the quality of your work will likely be much better.

Why Are You Procrastinated?

Intentionally or unintentionally, we are all guilty of wasting our time at some point in our life but when it comes to setting up a successful and profitable business, we must overcome our fears.

Even a simple task feels like it is very difficult when you doubt yourself. When you are dealing with self-doubt, you will end up finding a lot of reasons not to get something done because you keep thinking that you are going to fail.

Procrastination will drag you in the direction of failure. It will also stop you from fulfilling your dreams because if you're allowing negative thoughts and self-doubt to lead the way, you'll never have enough faith in your abilities to get things done. Procrastination has been identified as one of the closest things that leads you to underachievement.

A lot of people are affected by negativity and self-doubt so if you're going through the same, don't worry you're not alone. This feeling of negativity and self-doubt is a very common struggle with entrepreneurs around the globe.

The main reason why this feeling of negativity and self-doubt arises is when you see your competitors succeed. You compare yourself to them and wonder whether you have enough knowledge and skills to be in the same position as your competitors.

For example, if you are a teacher or coach, it is very easy to feel that you are not skilled or experienced enough to charge people for your information but that's all because of the negativity and self-doubt in your mind.

Deep down inside, you know that it's not true. You've probably worked hard to get to where you are and deserve every bit of the success you achieve. Overcoming those negative feelings will take some determination and will, but if you make the commitment to yourself and your business, and you stick to it, nothing will stop you from reaching your goals.

Don't let the negative feelings and self-doubt be your worst enemy and sabotage your efforts. Identify your weaknesses and focus on your strengths.

Commit to getting the tasks done every single day so that you're too busy achieving success in your industry and keep that negativity away from your goals. Focus on your work towards improving your workflow while letting go of those negative feelings.

No, it won't always be easy and it'll take a determined effort on your part, but if you work towards reprogramming your way of thinking, you'll vanquish those anti-success messages and reinvigorate that desire that made you take the leap from employee to self-employed in the first place.

You can do this!

Avoid Distractions

Earlier in this book, we talked about the importance of avoiding distractions. You now understand the effectiveness of sub-tasking and that by implementing this into your workweek you'll be able to use your time more efficiently and be more productive.

Your working environment is equally important as your workflow. You should make sure to separate your personal life from your work life, which means talking with friends and family who may feel that just because you're working from home, you're free for conversations throughout the day.

Set a routine for yourself and try to stick with it. If you can set a realistic work routine that everyone in your life understands, you'll be able to avoid distractions while making each hour count and be productive.

Doing this will also help you avoid burnout. You can only go full-speed ahead for so long before you'll suffer the consequences including a dried-up creative well. Pushing forward without breaks or any sort of normal schedule will also leave you scrambling to fix errors, revise projects, and will cause you to overlook important tasks.

You've likely been through this already. You work so hard on a project for so long that you end up forgetting important information, or overlook something that causes your project to fail.

As for your office environment itself, it all depends on what helps you to stay focused. For some, they find that music helps them focus while others need it to be completely silent. Do your best to figure out what kind of routine will get you into a working positive mindset.

Does working out in the morning help?

Do you have to shut off your phone, close your email, or fire up a playlist to spring into action?

Find what works for you and stick with it.

Your family, your mental health, your physical health, and your career will thank you for it.

Be Accountable

Hopefully, by now you already have ideas as to how to create an organized schedule that will boost productivity and help you use your time effectively. If not, make that your top priority.

And you're second priority should be to hold yourself accountable if you make any mistakes.

If you're struggling to get things done, it's easy to switch up the routine believing that will help you get back on track. However, if you take the time to analyze why are you making the mistake in the first place, chances are you'll be able to identify where things are going wrong and you'll be able to fix the mistake.

Take a step back and think about where and when your efforts went wrong.

Were you spending too much time on things like email or social media?

Did you fail at prioritizing your goals and ended up spending too much time on things with low priority?

Self-correcting and holding yourself accountable are two very important lessons when it comes to being successful in your business.

The key is to develop habits that help you to work and to play. It must sound strange but it not. Just like you need to figure out a way to get into work mode, you also have to develop habits that help you shut it down when your creativity or quality begins to decline.

It's way too easy to say "just a few more minutes", or to push through and get that "one more task done", but it does you no good if you end up having to do the task again because you were so burned out that you didn't give your very best effort. Your business deserves the best of you and so do your clients.

Holding yourself accountable isn't always easy, but it's the enemy of procrastination. If you take the time to identify where you went wrong, you'll stay clear of self-doubt by immediately correcting the issue and moving on.

Stop Being a Perfectionist

If you're a perfectionist, you will find yourself spending extra time tweaking and improving on things that don't add value to your business.

It's easy to get caught up in wanting everything to be perfect. This can also go hand-in-hand with those who struggle with procrastination. These two entrepreneurial struggles are like twins. You can't always tell them apart.

Overcoming being a perfectionist is one of the hardest things many of us will ever do because chances are, we've been like this our entire lives and not just professionally. We want things to be as great as they can be and we find it hard to settle for anything less.

When it comes to business, this can lead to delayed launches or projects that never get to market. We pick it apart, come up with new ideas or ways to constantly improve it.

Now don't get me wrong, being a perfectionist can be an incredible asset for us entrepreneurs because it also means that we won't just throw out lousy products or services just to be doing something.

At the same time, we need to learn to let go and that nothing will ever be perfect no matter how much time or energy we spend on it.

The key is to start looking at perfectionism as an enemy to your business. It will cost you money and time. Being perfect is impossible and putting out an error-free product or a service that doesn't ever encounter its share of hiccups is a myth.

One of the ways to improve productivity is to assign a time frame to each product either by days or hours and stick to it. Set a deadline for yourself and be ruthless in not allowing any changes to be made.

Taking action is the only way you'll ever get to the level of success that you deserve, so try to adopt the mindset that it doesn't have to be perfect, it just has to be done. Launched is better than being perfect and never launched.

An available product is better than a project sitting on your hard drive. Sure, there's always room to improve and you will, but only by being consistently productive and seeing things through.

To Summarise

We hope this book has given you a few different ideas as to how can you manage your time effectively and boost your day-to-day productivity.

We also hope it's given you a bit of encouragement because we all need it regardless of what business we're in.

Before saying goodbye, We'll leave you with a few tips that have will help you to stay on track and maximize the value of the time I spent on my business.

Don't be afraid of failure, failures Will Make You a Better Entrepreneur: It's hard to believe, but it's true. If you accept that despite the best-laid plans and the most detailed business strategy known to man, you're still going to encounter struggles and failures, then you'll become a better, more confident, and focused entrepreneur.

Set deadlines on everything: Just like we can easily go overboard with the time we spend on projects; we can equally do the same with our down-time. Try to create a balance between having a personal life and a consistent work one. Commit to a schedule and stick to it.

Prioritize important things: Perfectionists can easily waste a ton of valuable time by focusing on only one aspect of a project. Instead, work towards prioritizing your goals based on what's most important. Focus on getting that done and you won't struggle to meet deadlines or find yourself scrambling to get other things done because you spent too much time on just one thing.

That's all for now. Wish you the very best of success in your venture!

Printed in Great Britain
by Amazon

86174412R10016